Hamza Hates His Bed!

A Bedtime Book for Muslim Kids

by

Nimo Ali

Every night at bedtime, Hamza throws a fit. He pouts and shouts and stomps his little feet. He says, "No, no, no! I hate that bed!".

His mother tries to tell him how comfortable his bed is, but he refuses to listen.

"Feel how soft your pillow is!" says Hamza's mother. "I don't care how soft it is!" cries Hamza. "I don't want to sleep there!"

Hamza looks at his mother with sad eyes. "I want to sleep in your bed," he pleads.
"Hamza," replies Hamza's mother with a sigh. "Why do you hate your bed so much?"

Hamza hugs her tightly. "I'm scared to sleep by myself Mama," he whispers.

"You have Allah who is powerful," Hamza's mother tells him.
"Allah protects you while you sleep. He watches over you at
night."

"Just remember to do something very special before you
sleep. If you do, you will never feel scared again,
InshaaAllah!" comforts Hamza's mother.

"Come on. We will do what Prophet Muhammad told us to do before we sleep. That way, Allah will protect us all night, and we will not be afraid of anything. InshaaAllah!"

With her hands in front of her face, Hamza's mother recites Sura Al-Ikhlas three times, Sura Al-Falaq three times, and Sura Al-Nas three times. Then she blows on her hands three times.

Hamza also puts his hands in front of his face and recites Sura Al-Ikhlas, Sura Al-Falaq, and Sura Al-Nas three times each.

After she is done reciting, Hamza's mother rubs her hands all over her body, starting from her head and moving all the way down to her toes. Hamza copies her movements.

Then Hamza's mother starts reciting Ayatul Kursi, the greatest Ayah in the entire Qur'an!

Hamza has not yet learned to recite Ayatul Kursi, so he listens to his mother as she recites the greatest ayah in the entire Qur'an.

When Hamza's mother is finished, she makes more dua. "Ameen," she says.

Then she faces Hamza, holding his shoulders firmly. "You will be protected now. InshaaAllah."

Hamza nods his head. His eyelids grow heavy, and he puts his hand over his mouth to cover his yawn.

Before Hamza's mother can say another word, she notices he's sound asleep.

"What a good boy," she whispers as she kisses him on the forehead and pulls up his blanket.

"Goodnight son," Hamza's mother whispers, again.
"Asalaamu alaykum."

Very carefully, she tiptoes out of the room and closes the door.

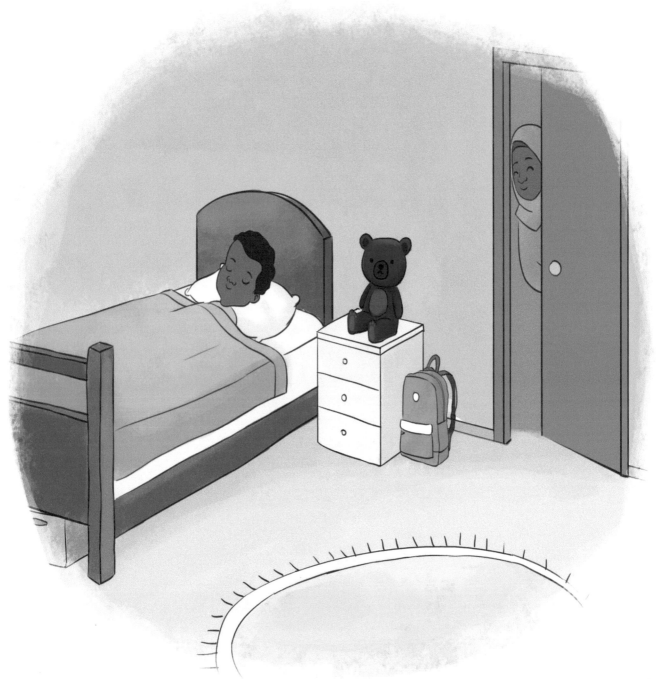

The End

TEST FOR UNDERSTANDING

1. In the beginning of the story, is Hamza happy or angry?

2. When Hamza hugs his mother, what does he whisper to her about how he feels going to sleep by himself?

3. What does his mother tell him to make him feel better?

4. What are the three suras that Hamza and his mother recite before going to sleep?

5. Who did Hamza's mother say taught Muslims to recite these suras/ayah before sleeping?

6. What is the greatest ayah in the entire Qur'an?

7. Do you get scared sometimes and was this story helpful to you?

Send any comments/questions or suggestions you may have about this story to the following email address:

loveAllahalways2015@gmail.com

Jazaakumulaahu Khayran!

AHADEETH ON SLEEP ETIQUETTES

It was narrated from 'Aa'ishah (may Allah be pleased with her) that when the Prophet (blessings and peace of Allah be upon him) went to his bed every night, he would put his cupped hands together, then blow into them, then recite into them Qul Huwa Allahu ahad, Qul a'oodhu bi Rabb il-Falaq and Qul a'oodhu bi Rabb il-Naas, then he would wipe his hands over as much of his body as he could, starting with his head and face, and the front part of his body. He would do that three times.
*The word translated here as 'blow' refers to spitting lightly and dryly.

Narrated by al-Bukhaari (5017).

It was narrated that Abu Hurayrah (may Allah be pleased with him) said: The Messenger of Allah (peace and blessings of Allah be upon him) put me in charge of guarding the collected zakaah of Ramadaan. Someone came and started to rummage in the food. I took hold of him and said, I will surely take you to the Messenger of Allah (peace and blessings of Allah be upon him). He [the one who came and rummaged in the food] said, When you go to your bed, recite Aayat al-Kursiy and you will be protected by Allah, and no devil will come near you until morning. The Prophet (peace and blessings of Allah be upon him) said, "He told you the truth even though he is a liar. That was a devil."

Narrated by al-Bukhaari (2311).

Hudhaifah (May Allah be pleased with him) reported: Whenever the Prophet (s) lay down for sleep at night, he would place his (right) hand under his (right) cheek and supplicate: "Allahumma bismika amutu wa ahya [O Allah, with Your Name will I die and live (wake up-)]." And when he woke up, he would supplicate:

"Al-hamdu lillahil-ladhi ahyana ba'da ma amatana, wa ilaihin-nushur (All praise is due to Allah, Who has brought us back to life after He has caused us to die, and to Him is the return)."

Narrated by Al-Bukhari

Ya'ish bin Tikhfah Al-Ghifari (May Allah be pleased with him) reported: My father said: I was lying down on my belly in the mosque when someone shook me with his foot and said, "Lying down this way is disapproved by Allah." I looked up and saw that it was Messenger of Allah (s).

Narrated by Abu Dawud

ABOUT THE AUTHOR

Nimo Ali is a Somali-American author and home schooling mother of six. She currently lives in the United States with her children. Her dream is to one day become a hafidah of the Qur'an, inshaaAllah. In her spare time, she loves to take nature walks with her family.

Other Books by Nimo Ali

Read other books by Nimo Ali

About the Story

Written in simple repetitive words that will hold and engage a young
child's attention, I Want to Be like Prophet Muhammad is the perfect
story to teach about, and encourage young children to emulate Prophet
Muhammad, salalaahu alayhi wassalam. After reading this story, your
children will want to be honest, caring, respectful, helpful etc. just like
Prophet Muhammad, inshaaAllah! This book is perfect for children
three years of age and older.

There are also ahaadeeth references as well as the
Prophet's full name in the index of the book.

I want To
Be Like
Prophet Muhammad
صَلَّى ٱللّٰهُ عَلَيْهِ وَسَلَّمَ

written
by
Nimo Ali

Illustrations
by
Amna Farooq
Fatima Naqvi

CPSIA information can be obtained
at www.ICGtesting.com
Printed in the USA
LVHW072055031122
732306LV00002B/141